You Have a Tube

Book Design: Brett Hillary Aronowitz

Copyright© 2016 by Brett Hillary Aronowitz

All rights reserved. No part of this book may be reproduced by any mechanical, photographic, or electronic process or in the form of a phonographic recording; nor may it be stored in a retrieval system, transmitted, or otherwwise copied for public or private use without prior written permission of the author.

The author of this book does not give medical advice or prescribe treatment for any physical, mental, or emotional conditions. The information in this book is intended to be of a supportive, educational nature and the author encourages those with health concerns to seek the attention of qualified health care practitioners. The author assumes no reponsibility for the action of her readers in this regard.

Library of Congress Control Number: 2017902359
ChickenScratchPress.com Van Nuys, CA 91405
ISBN: 978-1-7348204-7-8
Printed in the United States of America

For Dr. Philippe Jean Quilici
Thank you for fixing my tube

...and Astrid

Special thanks to an exceptional first grade teacher,
Marie Bernier Wheelock, who taught me that six year-olds
can understand complex concepts and spell words like *metamorphosis*.

The content of this book honors the intelligence of small children
who are capable of greatness when they are not repeatedly
drilled down with stupidity.

Dear Parents, Grandparents, and Caregivers;

As caretakers of children, one of our most important responsibilities is being their teacher. Children love to learn and want desperately to understand how this world works.

In fact, fiction may be a more difficult concept for children to understand than teaching them non-fiction. Why bombard them with fantasy and make-believe while they are just learning about how trees grow, where paper comes from, or what makes the waves at the beach. Everything about our world is new and deserves an explanation.

The subject most deferred and often ignored is perhaps the most important of all. How does our body work? Is it so complex that only doctors or other highly intelligent people can learn about it? Or is it because our reductionist world, a world of specialization, creates languages unfamiliar to the average person, thus separating people who know the language from those who don't.

When I was a child, Bob Dylan gifted my family with a set of Encyclopedia Britanica. What I remember most about these revered books was contained in the first volume. The anatomy listing included a series of colorful acetate overlays. By turning each acetate page, I revealed the underlying layer in the body, all the while creating a three-dimensional model in a two-dimensional space. Anatomy was both fascinating and terrifying, and all I was doing was looking at the pictures.

Many years later, when I began my chiropractic education, one of my first classes was an introduction into the vocabulary that separates doctors and other medical professionals from laypeople. The class was Medical Terminology. A knee was a patella. Laying on one's back was supine, and on one's stomach was prone. The first step in learning about the body was learning the language of doctors.

And so when I wrote *You Have A Tube*, I did so because of a medical crisis of my digestive system that nearly killed me. I did so because I have always believed that food is your best medicine and the three components that make up good health are nutrition, sleep and exercise. I wrote *You Have a Tube* because it occurred to me that next step after reading *Everyone Poops* by Taro Gomi was a book with more information--a basic anatomy and physiology reference book written for elementary students. A book that belongs in every classroom and in every home bookshelf. A book fascinating without being terrifying.

You Have A Tube empowers kids by teaching them about their bodies. The concept of a tube will inform and entertain even very young children, while the vocabulary will build on concepts of increasing complexity. A common reaction made by parents and teachers is, "I didn't know any of this."

I hope that the information and vocabulary presented in *You Have A Tube* will equip patients to discuss aspects of their digestive health with doctors in a meaningful way throughout their lives. My goal is to make it the first in a series of *You Have a Body* books.

To Your Health,

Brett Aronowitz

This is a tube.

Really…it is.

This is also a tube.

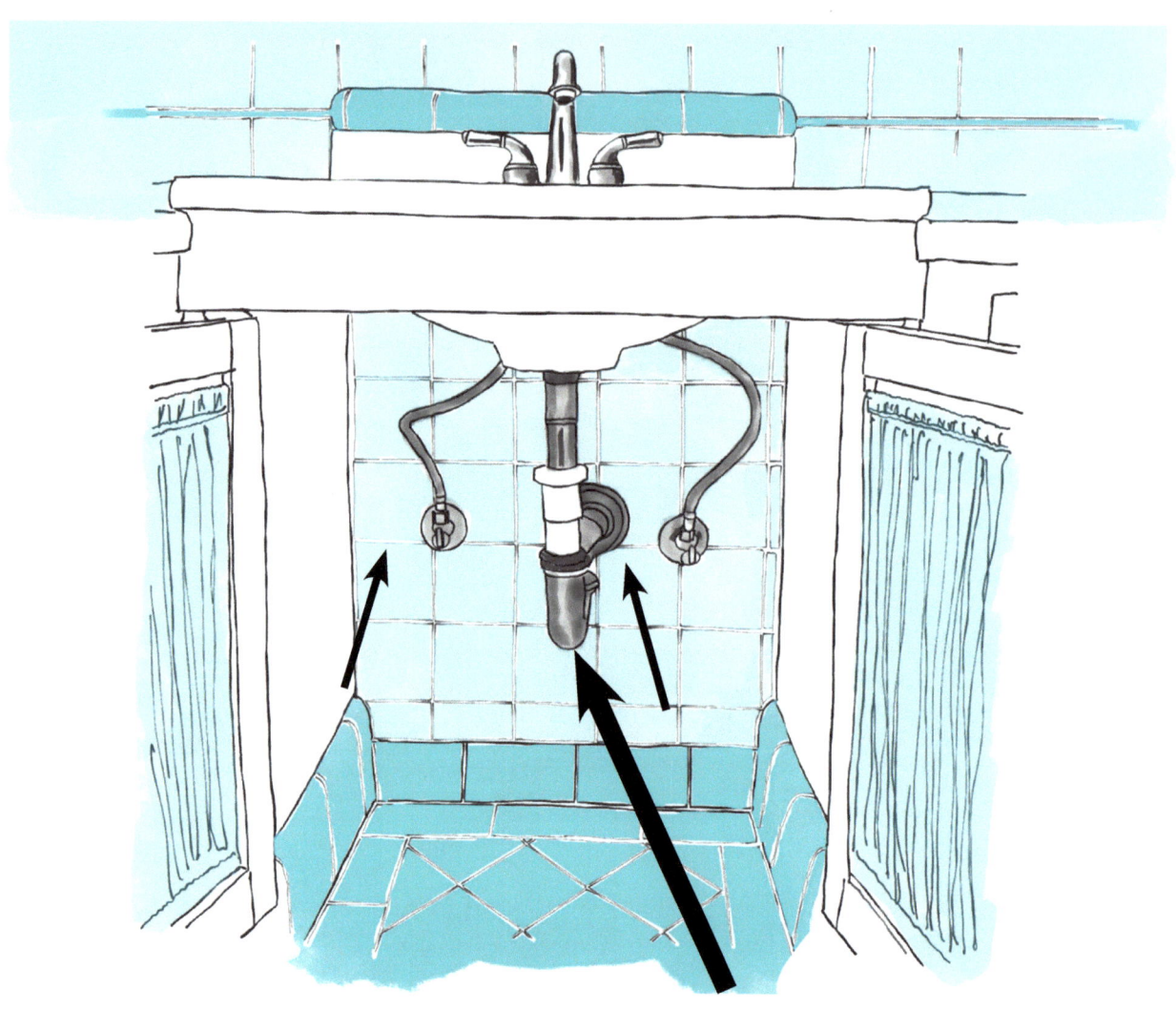

So is this
...and these.

Stuff goes in...

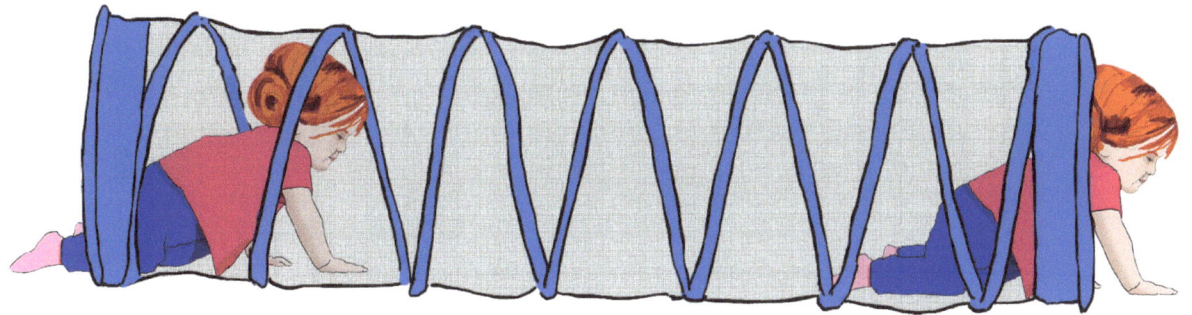

...and stuff comes out.

What makes a tube...a tube?
Stuff goes in ... and stuff comes out.

Which of these things is a tube?

You have a very important tube in your body that you use everyday.

You use it when you eat.
(Stuff goes in).

You use it when you poop.
(Stuff comes out)

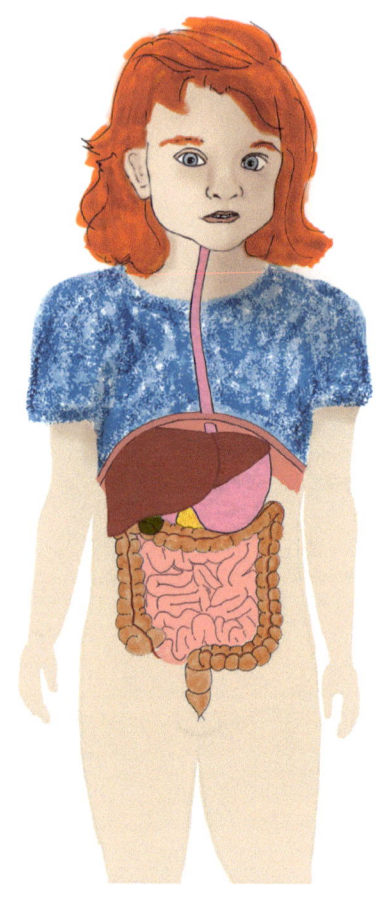

It's called the *digestive tract*,* but it's a tube. It's divided into different sections with big names. Parts of the tube take apart or break down the food while other parts absorb the food to give you energy. The whole process is called *digestion*.

*It's called a tract because other organs connect to it with their own tubes

CHEW YOUR FOOD WELL!

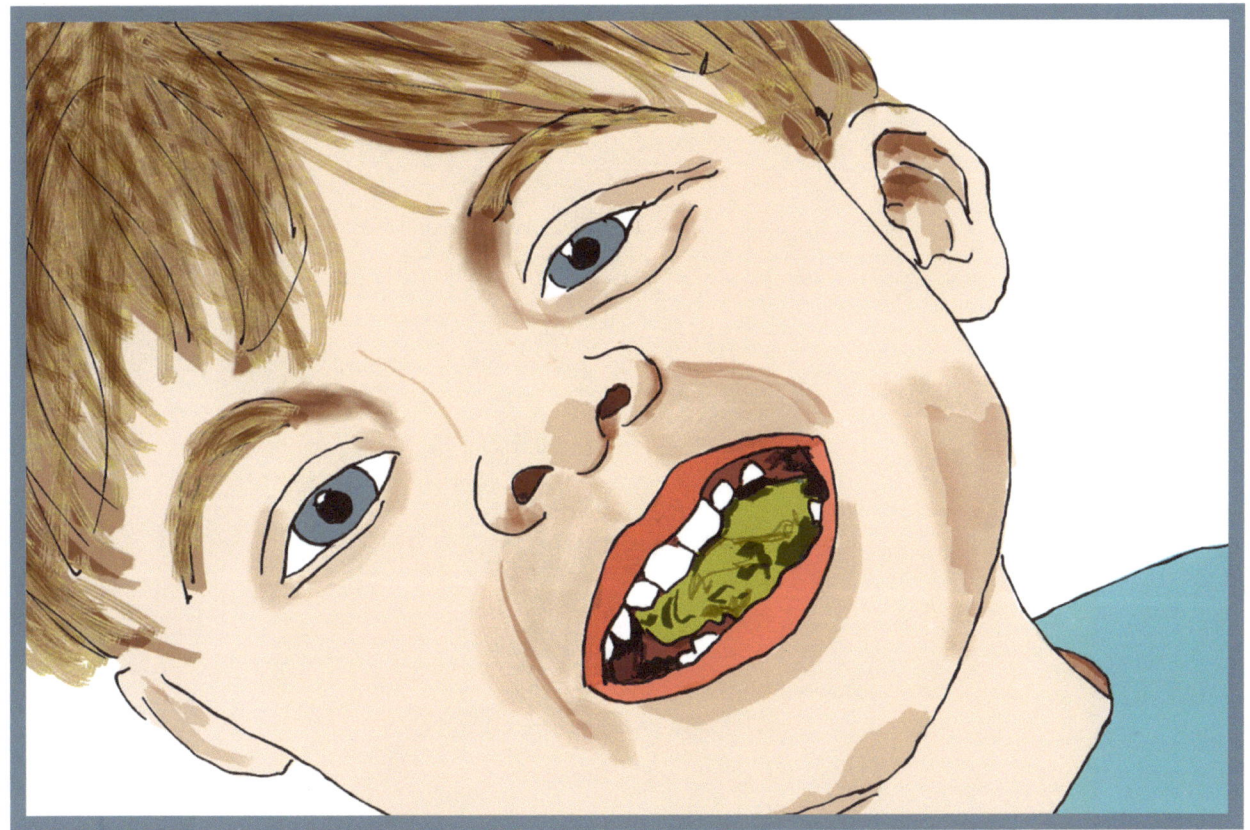

Your tube starts at your mouth and requires chewing—a lot of chewing. Chewing is also called *mastication*.

This is why you must take care of your teeth. You need them for digestion! Chew your food until it's almost a liquid and there's nothing left to chew.

Chewing mixes the food with your spit (also called *saliva*). *Saliva* contains special juices and enzymes that help digestion. Drinking water every day helps your digestion too.

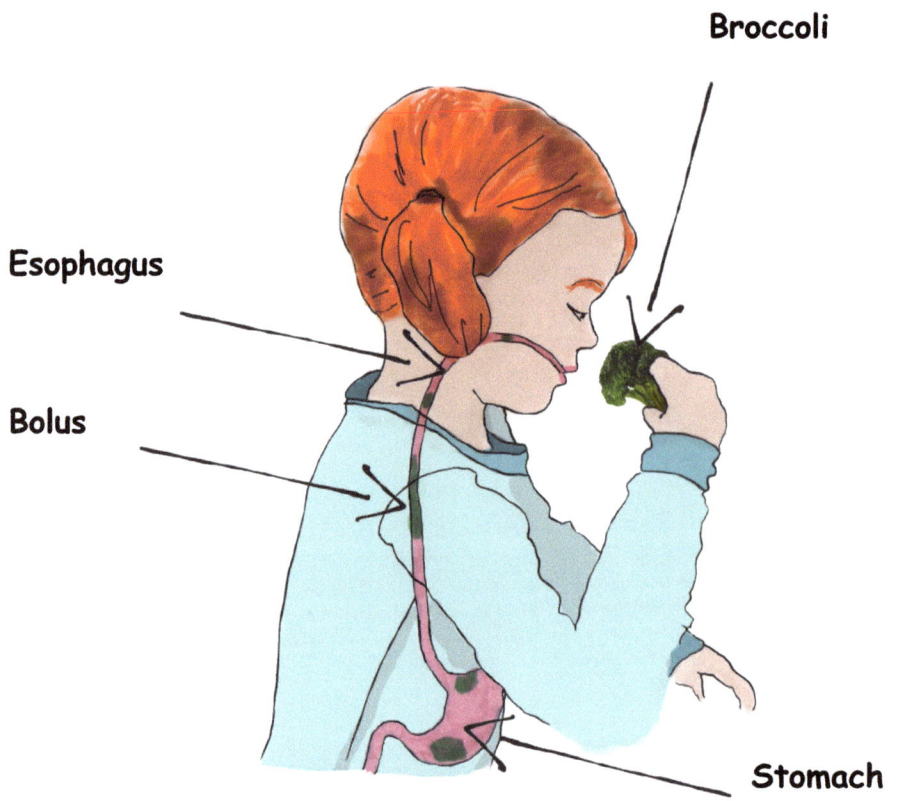

Chewing is important because it turns your food into a slippery slop called a ***bolus.*** When you swallow, the bolus slides easily down your throat, through a part of the tube known as the ***esophagus*** and lands in another part of the tube called the ***stomach***. The esophagus is lined with muscles that squeeze and push the bolus into the stomach.

ONLY EAT FOOD!

Only eat food.

Do not swallow other objects that could get stuck in the tube.

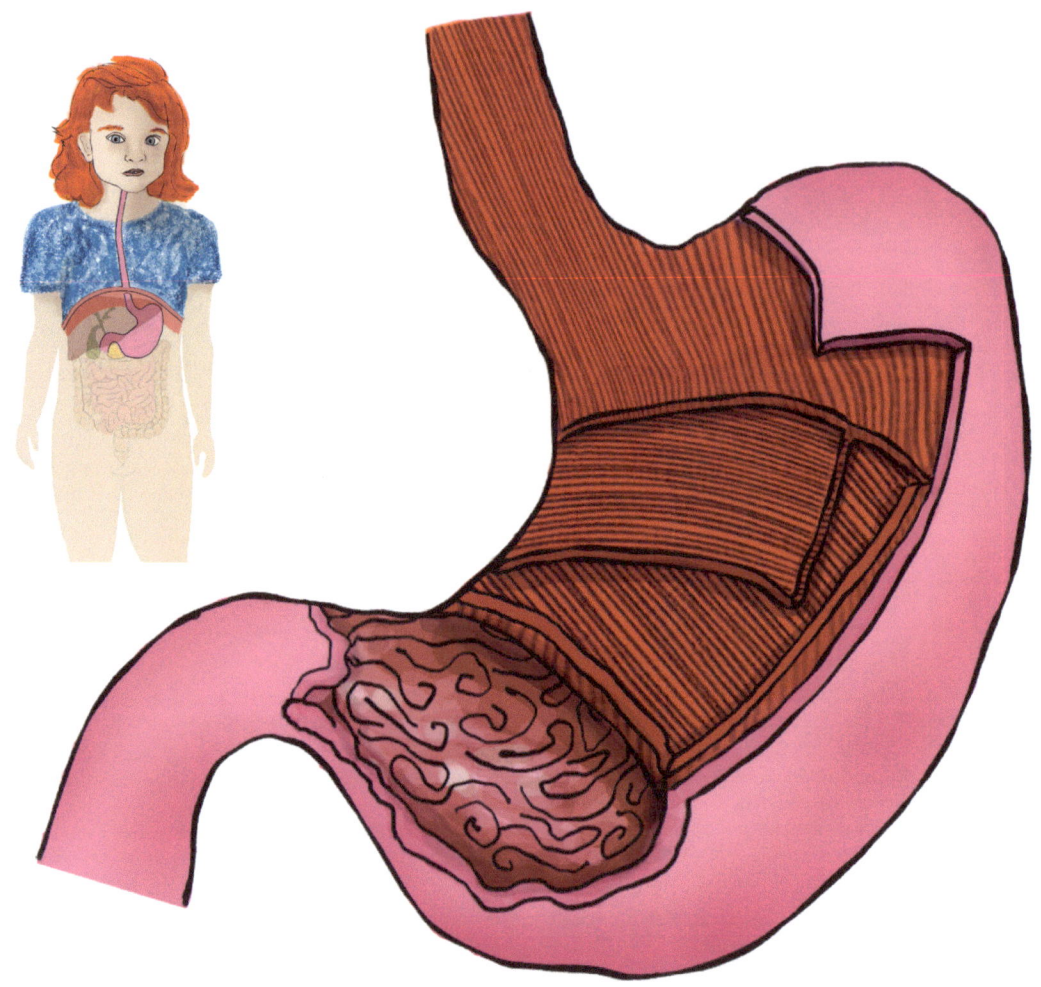

Three layers of muscle in the stomach squeeze and churn the bolus in different directions, mixing it with stomach acids and enzymes that break down the food. Acids* are very strong.

*When you vomit, that horrible taste is from the acids.

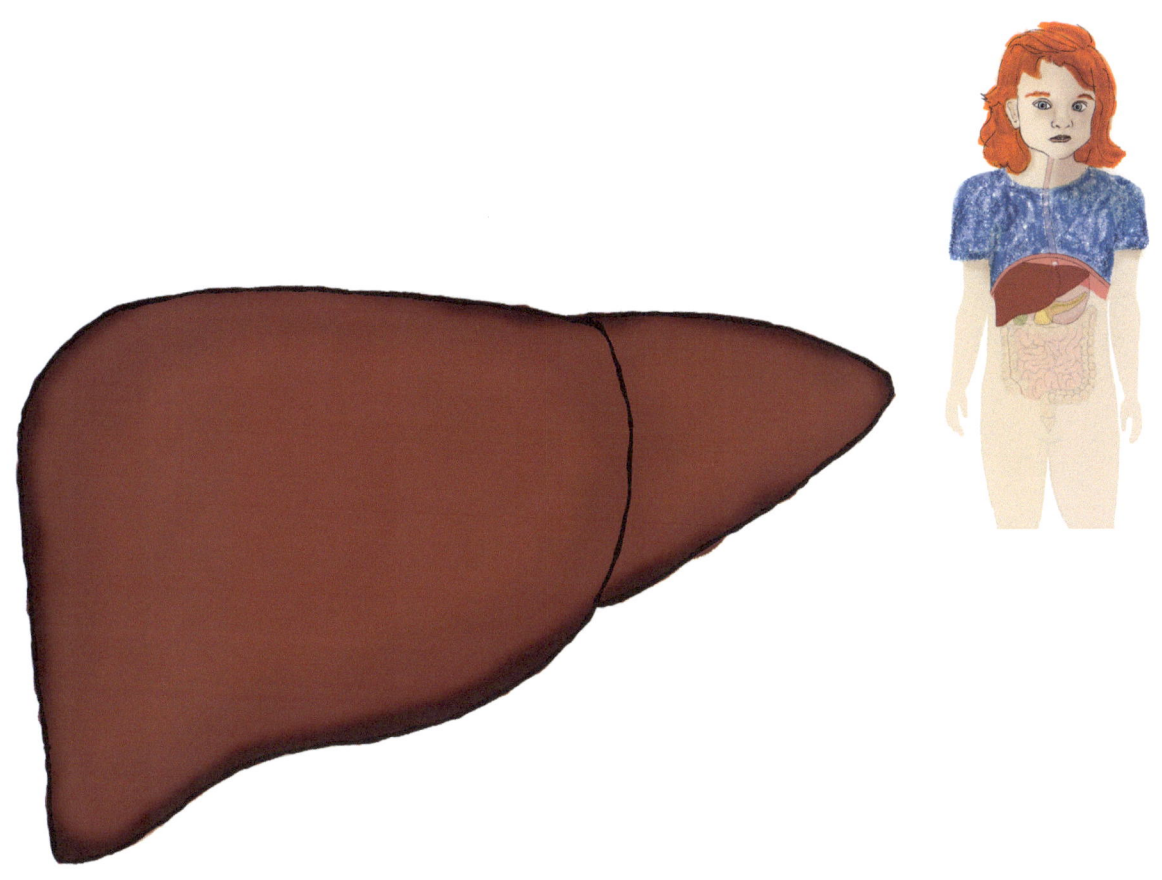

The *liver* produces a liquid called *bile* which helps to digest fats. It sends the bile through a tube, to a storage center called the *gallbladder*.

Ice cream, avocados, coconut and olives all have fat. Which is your favorite?

    The *gallbladder* holds the bile until you eat food with fat in it. Most foods have some fat. The bile is then released into the small intestine through its own tube.

    The body is very smart.

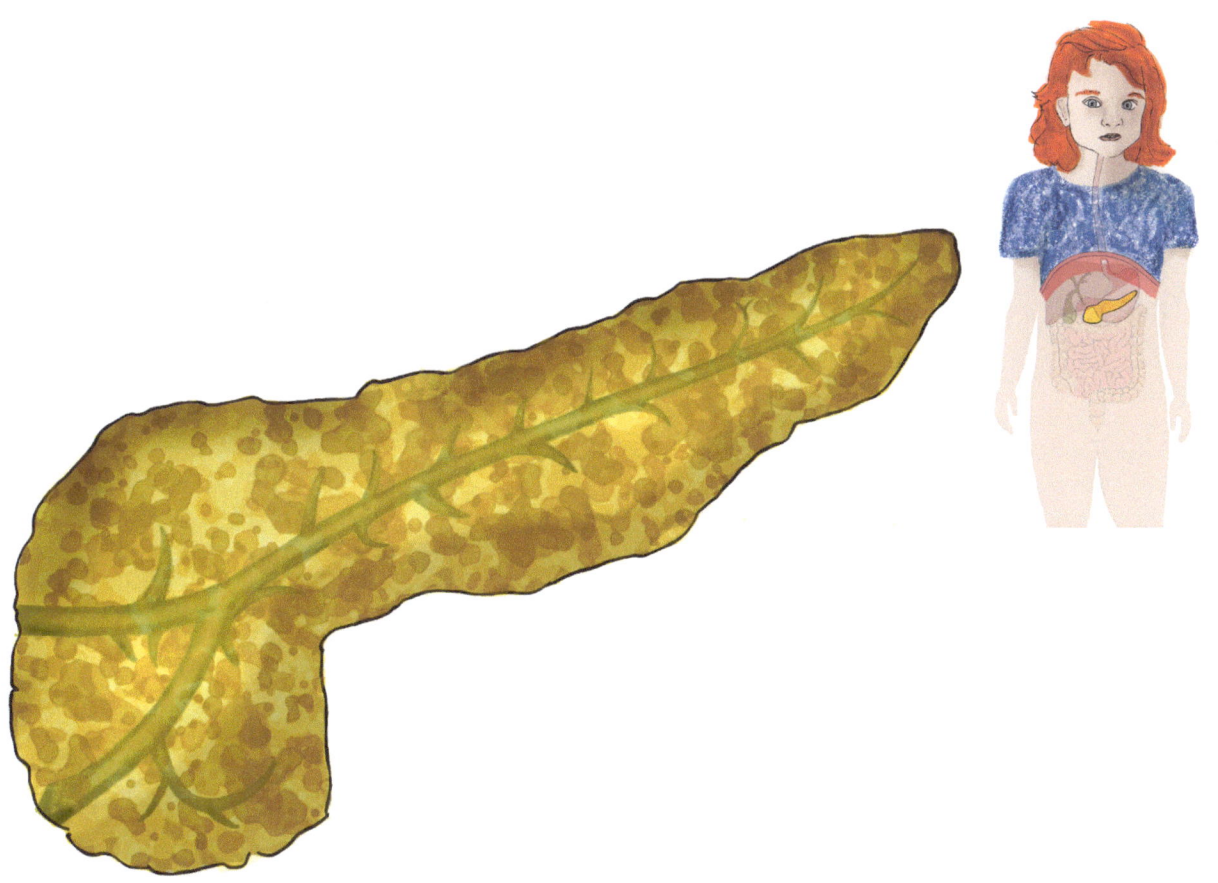

The *pancreas* also makes enzymes which help turn food into tiny parcels of energy used to repair the body and keep it healthy. Can you guess how the pancreas releases the enzymes?

If your answer was "through a tube," you are correct!

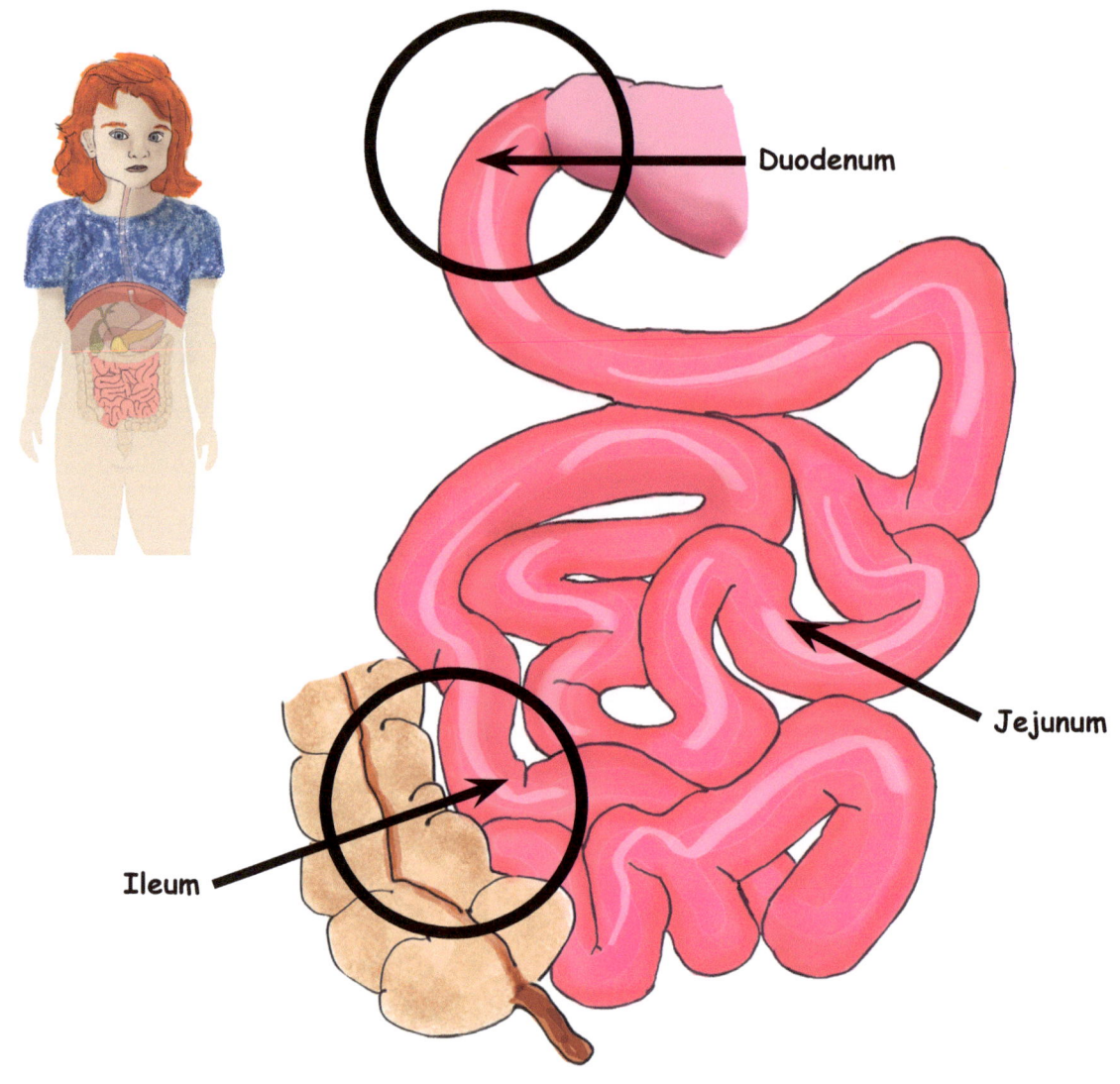

As the bolus leaves the stomach, it is now called *chyme*. Chyme enter the *duodenum,* which is the first of three parts of the *small intestine.* The *jejunum* is the middle portion and the last part is the *ileum* which attaches to the large intestine.

The small intestine absorbs the food you eat.

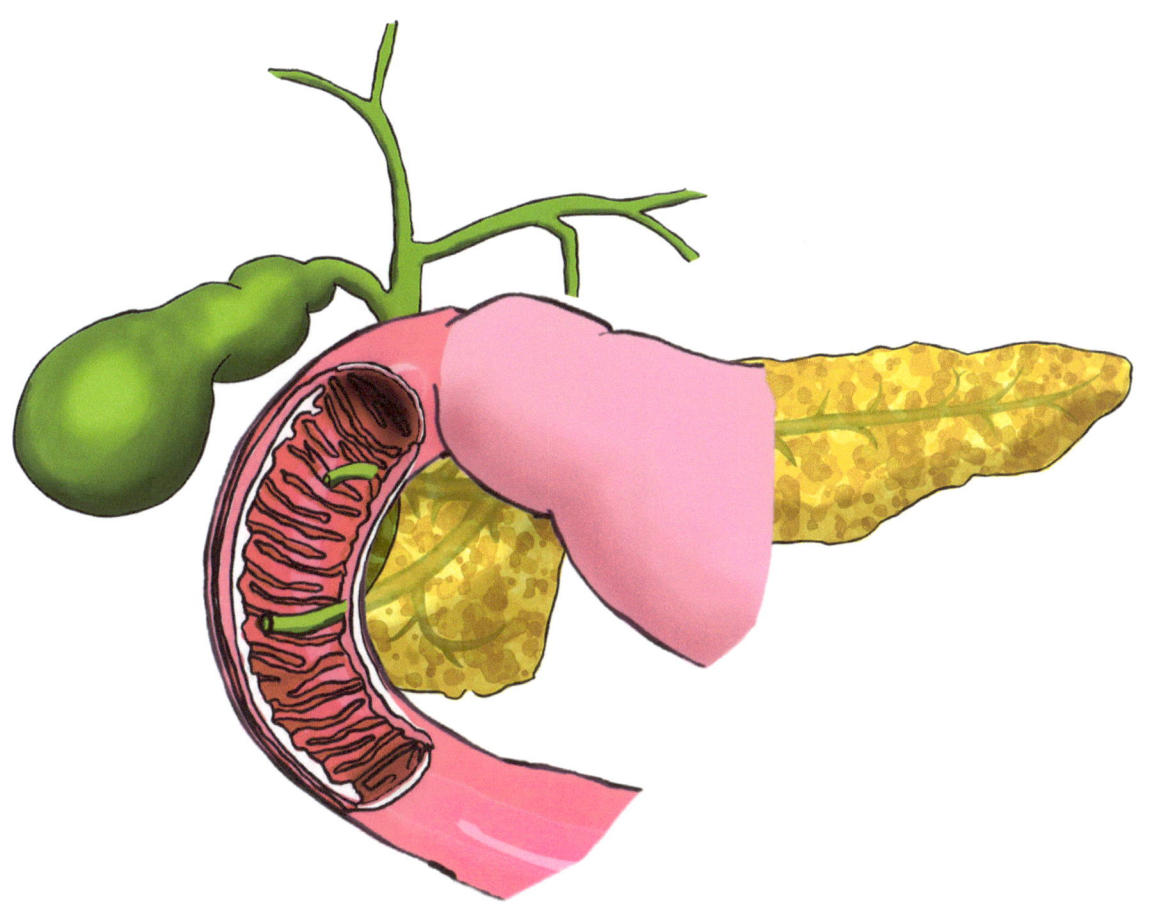

    Tubes deliver bile and enzymes from the gallbladder and pancreas to the duodenum to mix with the chyme. Digestion is completed in the duodenum and then nutrients are absorbed in the jejunum. The ileum pulls out bile acids and sends them back to the liver to be reused to make bile. The ileum also absorbs vitamins. Muscles in the small intestine help move the chyme down the tube.

When all the useable energy bits are absorbed in the small intestine, the waste products are left behind and the body must get rid of the trash.

So the garbage goes into the large intestine, which is called the *colon*. The colon also has three different parts with big names that mean simple things.

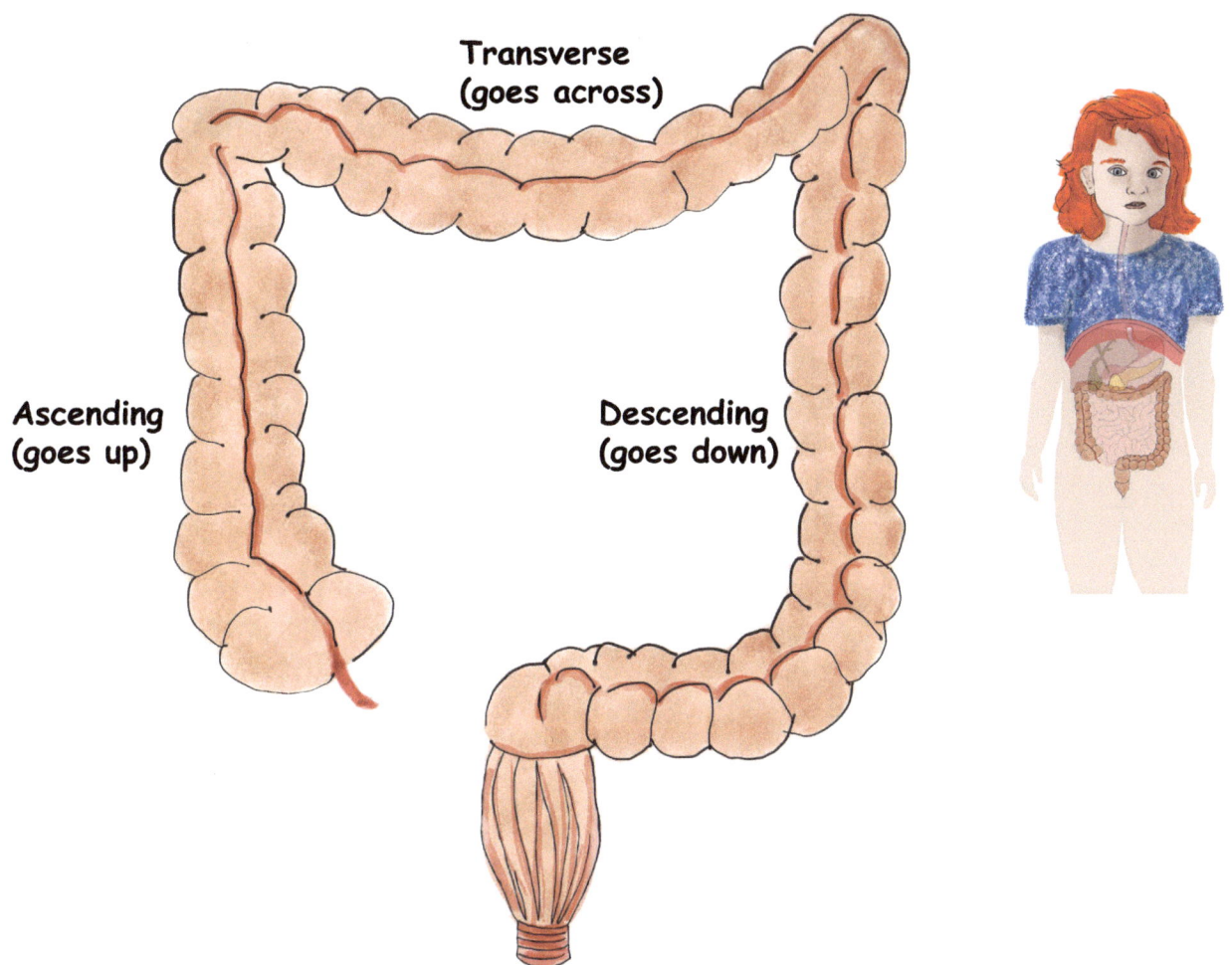

The *large intestine* pulls the water out of the trash along with other recycleable things like salts. What's left behind is your poop.

When you get sick, sometimes the large intestine doesn't work so well and you can get *diarrhea* (watery poop) or *constipation* (hard poop).

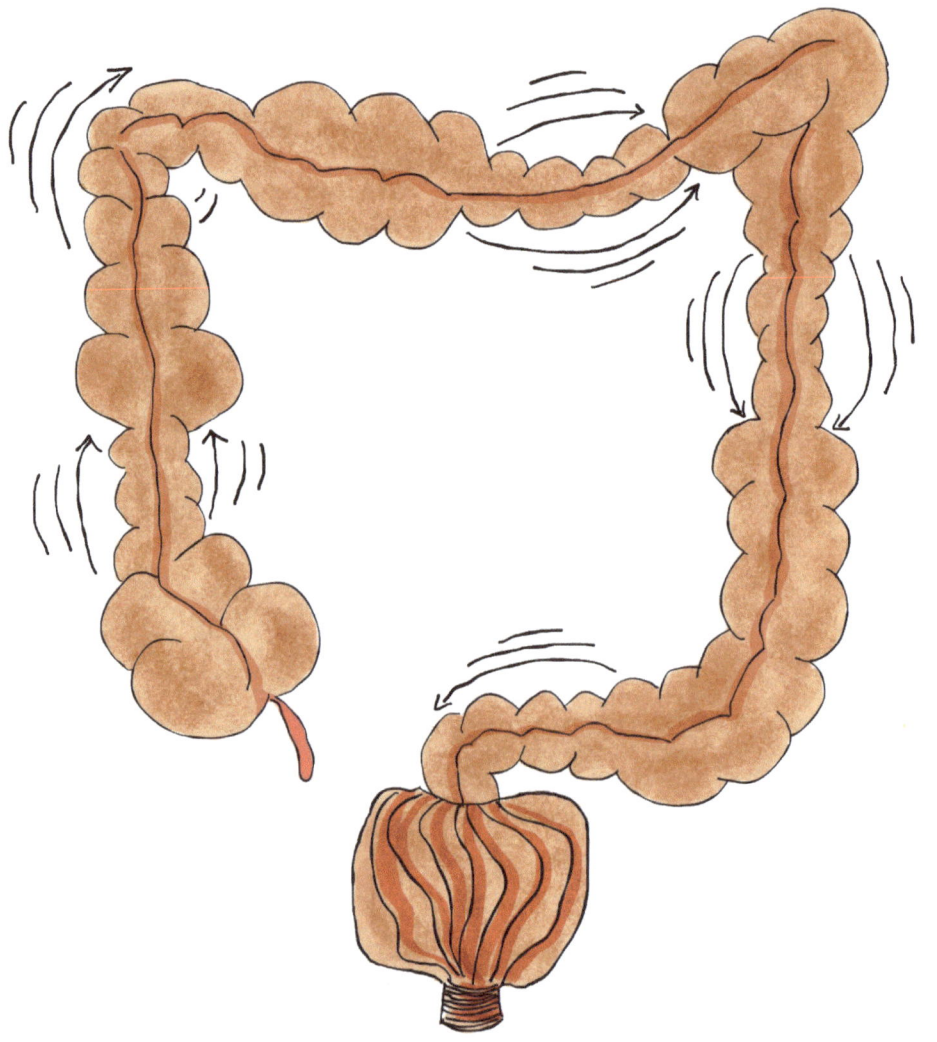

    Muscles in the large intestine tighten in wave-like movements pushing the poop through the tube. This is called *peristalsis*. Eating causes this to happen.

    Have you ever noticed that sometimes when you eat a meal, you have to go to the bathroom?

The end of the tube is called the rectum. When poop collects in the rectum, your body tells you with a very special feeling called an *urge*.

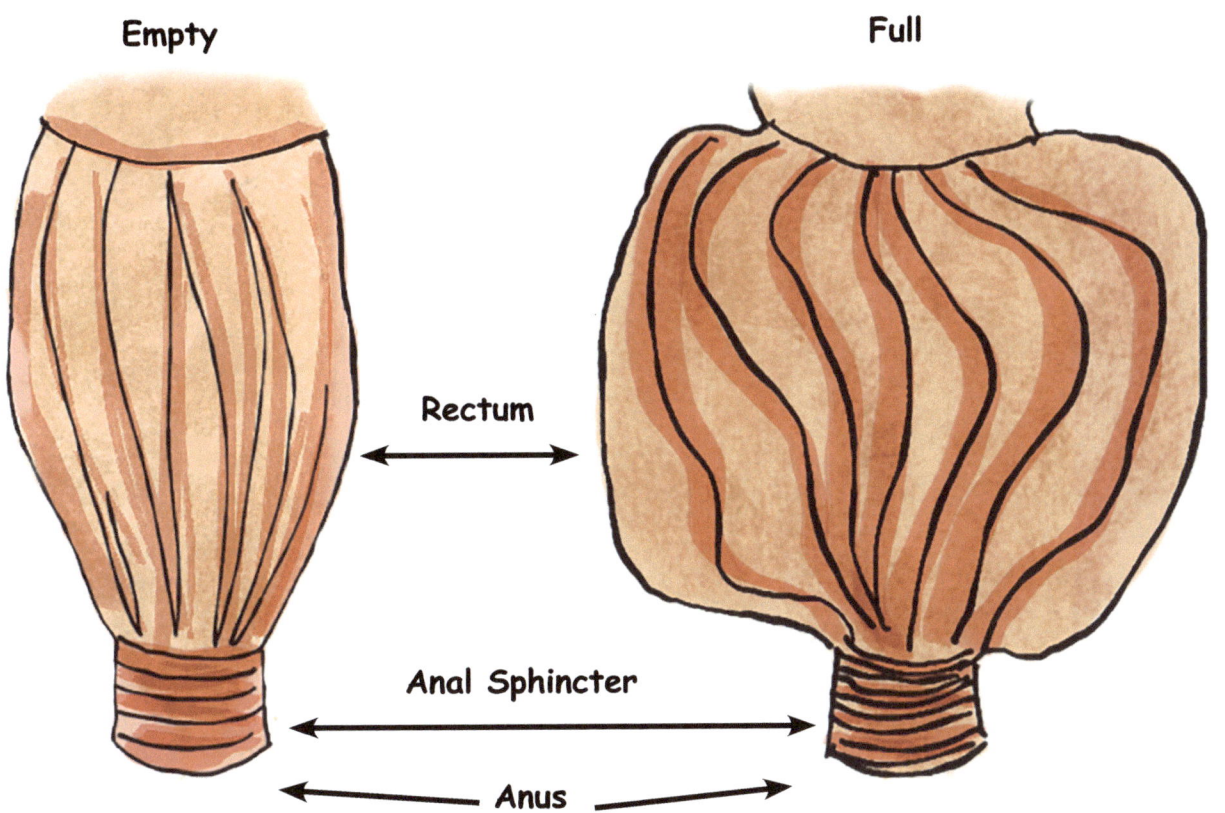

Thankfully, there is a very strong muscle called a ***sphincter***, holding the tube closed until you get to the toilet and relax. The end of the tube that opens to the outside of your body is called the ***anus***. When you have the urge to poop, get to a bathroom as quickly as you can. Holding your poop isn't so good for your body.

If you stretch out the entire digestive tube, it is about twenty feet long (thirty feet in grown ups), which is roughly the distance from one side of the street to the other.

How long does it take for food to travel through the tube? It's different for each person.

The amount of time it takes for food to move from your mouth to the toilet is called your *transit time*.

There's a way you can find out your transit time. It's called an *experiment*. The most important part of this experiment is to use your sense of observation.

Have your Mom (or Dad) cook some red beets. An easy way to is to bake them in the oven like a potato. Eat your beets. Observe their bright color and sweet flavor. Notice what time you are eating them. The next part of the experiment is the hard part. You have to wait. In fact, you may have to wait a whole day or more, so don't forget about the experiment!

When you have the urge to poop, remember to look at it before you flush. Did you notice anything unusual? How much time passed since you ate the beets? What color was your poop? Different foods can change the color of your poop and alter your transit time.

How your body works is one of the most important things you can learn in your lifetime. Become an expert, know about the foods you eat, and how they affect your body and your transit time.

There are many other tubes in the body. Some of them don't open to the outside like the digestive tract. Can you guess what they may be?

Learning New Words!

If you have trouble pronouncing these terms, go to http://www.oxfordlearnersdictionaries.com/us/about/pronunciation_english and type in the words:

digestion	pancreas	descending
digestive tract	chyme	diarrhea
mastication	small intestine	constipation
saliva	duodenum	peristalsis
bolus	jejunum	rectum
esophagus	ileum	urge
stomach	large intestine	sphincter
liver	colon	anus
bile	ascending	transit time
gallbladder	transverse	experiment

www.ingramcontent.com/pod-product-compliance
Lightning Source LLC
Chambersburg PA
CBHW040736150426
42811CB00064B/1706